TAKE THE LEAD

• Heather Watson •

with illustrations by
Libby Drew

Whittet Books

First published 1998
Text © 1998 by Heather Watson
Illustrations © 1998 by Libby Drew

Whittet Books Ltd, Hill Farm, Stonham Rd, Cotton, Stowmarket,
Suffolk IP14 4RQ

British Library Cataloguing in Publication Data. A catalogue
record for this book is available from the British Library.

ISBN 1 873580 40 1

Printed and bound by Bookcraft

In fondest memory of Edward

ACKNOWLEDGMENTS

I am immensely grateful to my wonderful mother, Penny Watson, and great friend, Cordy Maling, who helped this book come to fruition.

I would like to express a considerable thank you to:

My grandfather, Jack Grattan, and to Jil Stein, both of whom have consistently supported me through the use of their premises.

All the staff at the Pines Veterinary Clinic, Maidenhead, Berkshire, and the Veterinary Healthcare Group, Berkshire, for their continued support and the use of their facilities.

All my friends for their much appreciated encouragement.

All my clients and especially their dogs, and all the dogs I have come to know, love and train for giving me inspiration and enthusiasm.

CONTENTS

FOREWORD

When we bring a dog into our home, in his eyes we are inviting him to join our pack and he will play by those pack rules – although as humans we often don't!

Using subtle domination in the way we run our everyday lives and learning to interact and communicate with our dogs on their level will help them to lead a more relaxed and content existence.

Understanding your dog's needs and how he thinks will enhance your relationship and lead to easier training.

Dogs, as pack animals, have a considerable inherent willingness to please, which is one of the reasons we have been able to domesticate them so easily.

By simply showing you are pleased with your dog when he is doing anything right, rather than being too concerned with his problems, you will enhance this valuable characteristic and make your pack life together considerably more enjoyable.

INTRODUCTION

Dogs have given the human race loyalty, companionship and pleasure for centuries. This wonderful friend, who can bring so much joy, can also be troublesome at times.

What we consider as a successful relationship is understanding your dog and his needs, thus making your relationship with your dog a happy one and ultimately making him easier to train.

What we often consider as inappropriate behaviour can be easily solved, or better still avoided, by giving your dog a clear understanding of how you would like him to behave and by reinforcing his good behaviour.

1 PACK HIERARCHY

Evidence suggests the dog is a direct descendant of the wolf and is most definitely a pack animal. When we bring a dog into our home, we invite him into our pack, and he will play by those pack rules – although as humans, we often don't.

As pack animals, dogs are social creatures relying on others around them for their mental well-being. A pack forms a strong family bond with the back-bone of its existence being a dominance order.

The word dominance often discourages dog-owners from looking at this side of dog training. It suggests you should tell your dog off and nag continually to control him. This, however, is not the case.

Simple and subtle domination of your dog in everyday life will give him security and stability.

By taking on the role of pack leader, you will take the burden of responsibility away from your dog, making him happier and more relaxed with the confidence that you are in control of his life and are able to protect him. By having this respect your dog will feel less need to question your authority, and will want to please you whenever he can.

Whenever possible, all members of the family should train, control, handle, play, feed and walk him as this will help him to be more adaptable and relaxed with his role in the pack.

Each individual should try to be consistent within himself; your dog will quickly build associations with different pack members.

The higher ranking the pack member, the more privileges it is allowed. Influencing a few activities in your home will greatly improve your overall control and keep you naturally and subtly in the alpha/top dog position.

Jumping up

When a dog jumps up at you or other people, although he may not be aware of it, he is in fact demonstrating and learning dominance: he is making his body posture larger, as he lunges towards you. (see Jumping Up – Chapter 5)

Mouthing

Your dog will mouth in play and to promote jaw and teeth development, but if your dog is mouthing you, he will learn he can inadvertently dominate. (see Mouthing – Chapter 5)

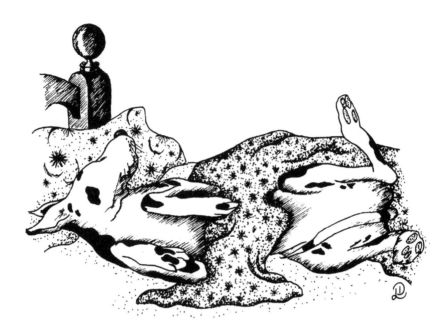

Sleeping arrangements

If your dog sleeps where he likes when he likes, this will
naturally elevate his position in the pack. It is totally up to you if
you like having your dog on the sofa for a cuddle or sleeping
next to you on your bed, but he should be invited up onto this
furniture by you, and not go when he decides to do so himself.
(see Jumping on Furniture – Chapter 5)

A dog should also have his own bed and be taught to go
onto it on command, as this can not only be a valuable control
method but will also give your dog a positive and secure
location. A blanket or bed can easily be moved from room to
room as and when required.

If you do allow your dog upstairs, it is a good idea to have at
least one family room that he is not allowed in – for example,
the dining room – as this again will subtly dominate and
naturally keep him mentally beneath all members of the family.

Feeding

The alpha or top dog will always eat first, so it is important that
your dog eats last in the family. Dogs only think for the moment
so you need to disassociate your dog's feeding time with your
meal times. Do not feed him as you are just about to sit down for
your own meal, as this will encourage him to beg. Feed him a
little while before you eat, or wait until you have eaten.

If you would like to feed your dog left-overs or scraps, this is
fine (bearing in mind the nutritional values of the scraps, and
limiting amounts of extra food); but you should scrape these into
his bowl and feed him when all the family has finished.

By feeding your dog continually through a meal you are
encouraging him to beg. Begging is a dominance based activity
as your dog is looking at you demanding some food. If this
happens, take control and vocally command him to his bed ('In
your bed').

Using some simple obedience at feeding times will build a subtle domination and help you to stop him stealing. Get him to sit/stay (without physically controlling) and place his bowl in front of him, then tell him when he can start to eat.

From the start, all members of the family should regularly stroke your dog whilst he is eating. Putting your hand into his bowl and releasing something more exciting than his usual dinner, as a regular exercise practised by all family members, will help to reverse any protective tendencies. If you encounter any problems. (see Aggression – Chapter 5)

Doorways and stairs

Your dog pushing past you in a doorway or narrow gap is a dominance based activity – he is physically pushing you out of the way and is going first: making a statement of leading the pack. Similarly, a dog that dashes up the stairs past you, then stands at the top looking down towards you is learning that he can dominate, as you are displaying a classic submissive body posture as you walk up the stairs towards him.

With any narrow passage or gap, your dog should walk behind you. Simply use your leg to stop him pushing past you.

* Make your dog sit/stay at the bottom of the stairs, then call him up, or make him walk behind you.
* Use simple obedience control if your dog is on the lead when walking out of your house or front gate. Vocally command your dog to sit/stay, then step through the door yourself. Turning to face your dog can help to reinforce this; call him through when you are ready.

Attention-seeking

When your dog demands affection, attention or games, he is showing dominance: he is trying to dictate to you what you should be doing at that time. (see Attention Seeking – Chapter 5)

Your dog needs to regularly interact with all members of the family. You can cuddle, stroke or play with him as much as you please but games, physical affection and attention should be started and ended on your terms, and not when he feels the need to be entertained.

If this is achieved on a casual basis your dog will relate to this method and be relaxed and stable, as a dog allowed to attention seek will become more and more demanding; this will eventually cause him to become insecure.

• As your dog comes to you for attention, give him the command 'off' or ask him to go to his bed. As he walks away from you, vocally praise him to reassure him, then call him back when you are ready (this can even be a few minutes later – as long as it is on your terms).

Dominance-based physical games such as tug of war can be played with your dog, but as this activity relates to fighting over food, the most dominant dog will always win. So, letting your dog win sometimes or ripping the item physically out of his mouth will only encourage a conflict, as you are backing down or inviting him to fight harder. Therefore, teach him to drop on command as this will subtly dominate. (see Dropping Items – Chapter 5)

2 HOW YOUR DOG THINKS

The cortex of a dog's brain is reasonably undeveloped compared to that of humans. The cortex deals with mental reasoning ability, planning and deliberate action. Therefore the dog only actually has the ability to *think for the moment.*

This, after all, is what makes dogs such wonderful companions and friends.

They cannot worry about the future, brood over the past, hold grudges or invent hidden meanings into others' intentions.

Their thought process is pure, displaying the emotion they feel at that time whether it is excitement, pleasure or fear.

Your consideration of this fact will make your dog so easy to understand and train.

A dog can only learn from direct experience and his memory is formed from pleasant and unpleasant associations. It is therefore important to build the correct associations in order to convey to your dog what you would like.

A dog will learn from habit, so by achieving a pattern of behaviour from an early age your dog will have a lasting association in his mind; for example, teach him to chew a bone when visitors are in the house; then later as people arrive he will go and find a toy to entertain himself.

Unfortunately this can also be a disadvantage as a dog will learn from his own behaviour, so do not be fooled that he will 'grow out of it!'

The timing of your commands is important when you are trying to train or educate your dog, so he can understand what is right and wrong.

For example: a dog chewing a table leg should be told that it is unacceptable behaviour, but the second he takes his mouth off the table leg, he must be told he is good. This will enable him to understand the association between right and wrong that you were trying to build.

If you come home and find a chewed article and show this to your dog, shouting your disapproval, he will only associate you finding the destroyed item as wrong, not the fact that he chewed it in the first place and he will feel increased anxiety when you are returning home.

Ignoring your dog, shutting him outside or continually telling him off will only cause confusion and start to break down his trust in you as no association has been built in his mind.

• You can only tell your dog off if you catch him doing something wrong. Otherwise you must act normally – as any disapproval you show would be inappropriate.

As soon as he stops, praise him, not only to build that association but also to mentally balance him to minimise any worry.

As a dog only learns from associations, your attitude is very important. You convey an attitude to your dog, so, for example, if he is excitable, you should be calm and clear. If you want to excite your dog to play, then you must act in that way too.

If your dog shows nervousness or anxiety in any situation, being over-supportive or praising him will only reinforce the behaviour he is showing, whereas a confident attitude will give him confidence: reassure when he is calm or ask him to sit, then praise him.

COMMUNICATION WITH YOUR DOG

Understanding how dogs communicate with each other gives us the key to how we should convey our intentions to them.

Dogs communicate by a combination of:

- Body posture
- Eye contact
- Sounds
- Physical actions

Body posture and eye contact are the two most important lines of communication.

A dominant body posture.

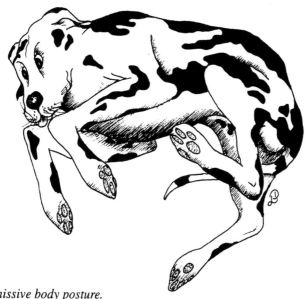

A submissive body posture.

Body posture

The larger a dog makes itself, the more dominant and
challenging it is being.

The smaller a dog makes itself, the more submissive it is
being – here it is taking a passive role.

Eye contact

Eye contact will be used in conjunction with body posture.

A direct stare from a dog that is showing a dominant body
posture is challenging you, whereas a more submissive dog will
avert its gaze as much as possible.

A dog showing a submissive body posture but using direct
eye contact is frightened.

Dogs use sound expressions and physical actions, such as
barking, whining, tail wagging and paw giving, to exaggerate
their communication.

When interacting with your dog, follow this simple guide:

Body posture

• If you are giving your dog a command or trying to assert some dominance over him, stand upright, with your shoulders straight – he will be much more likely to listen to you.
• If you want your dog to play or you want him to come to you, bend down as this will encourage him towards you.

Eye contact

• Look at your dog when giving commands or when reprimanding, as this will subtly dominate.

Physical gestures

• Use physical gestures in conjunction with your body posture and vocal command – it may help your dog to understand your intentions. For example: point to his bed when asking him to go in it. Point to the floor when you want him to lie down.

VOCAL COMMANDS

Your dog understands your tone of voice rather than the spoken word, although over a period of time he will recognise commonly used commands. Tone is the primary factor, and should convey your pleasure or disapproval.

* *If you are pleased with your dog sound it.*
* *If you give a command be assertive and positive.*
* *When you reinforce a command or reprimand your dog, be assertive and firm.*
* *Try to avoid shouting at your dog in close proximity, it can be quite disturbing (dogs have very sensitive hearing).*

To make education and training consistent, you should pick a command for each action you would like your dog to obey.

Command	Vocal tone	Use for	Body posture/eye contact
SIT	short, clear, positive	general control when excitable	stand upright, look at your dog
STAND	clear, reassuring	grooming vet checks	bend over slightly
DOWN	slow, commanding	general control for domination	point to the floor
STAY	firm, reassuring	general control for domination	stand upright, look at your dog
COME	encouraging, positive	recall	bend down
LEAVE IT	commanding and sharp	stealing picking things up unwanted sniffing	stand upright, look at your dog
DROP	commanding but positive	retrieve dropping items	stand upright, look at your dog
QUIET	calm and firm	barking winging	stand upright, look at your dog
OFF	firm, commanding	jumping up unwanted contact attention seeking	stand upright, look at your dog
IN BED	commanding and positive	general control positive location when excitable	stand upright, point at bed

When your dog is doing something inappropriate, it is probably because you haven't told him what he should be doing in that situation.

For example:

- 'in your bed' when he is fussing around your visitors.
- 'sit' at any time your dog is getting over-excited.
- 'leave it' when attempting to steal food or any inappropriate item.
- 'quiet' when barking.

As your dog only learns from association, it is also important to build the right association.

If he is doing something right praise him (even if you haven't asked him to do that action) – he will be more likely to respond and repeat this.

Always look at the positive aspects of your dog's behaviour and reinforce these rather than giving him all the attention when he is doing something wrong.

When using praise decide whether physical or vocal praise would be more appropriate at that particular time.

For example:

• If your dog is attention-seeking, use vocal praise once he has settled down or when he moves away as physical praise will only encourage him to attention seek more.
• If your dog is over-excited to see you or visitors, vocal praise would be more appropriate as physical praise will make him more excited.
• If your dog has returned quickly when you have called him, physical praise would be more appropriate to encourage such enthusiasm another time.

To build the correct association

Your timing is very important:

• *Ask your dog to do the required action in a positive and encouraging manner.*
• *Praise him whilst he is doing it.*

If your dog ignores you

- *Repeat the command in a firmer tone.*
- *Reinforce the action. For example: push your dog into a sit. Take your dog to his bed.*

Effective reinforcement is vital. Continual repetition of commands will only teach your dog he does not have to obey on the first command. Therefore, the timing of your command is very important.

How to tell your dog off

Since humans are smarter than dogs, using mental domination will be a more effective and a kinder way rather than physical force to ensure obedience.

When using subtle domination effectively you will find less need to reprimand your dog; if you do need to tell him off, he will be more likely to listen to you.

Any physical contact with your dog when he has done wrong will only encourage him to fight back and physically dominate you or defend himself, e.g. biting.

Reprimanding your dog through physical contact is not the answer; it will also undermine the other members of the family who may not have the capability to dominate in this way.

When telling your dog off use:

- A firm tone of voice
- A dominating body posture
- Eye contact
- Simple obedience commands – 'sit' or 'down' (to subtly dominate)

Exaggerate this if required by holding your dog under the chin and using your eye contact to dominate him, repeat your vocal command in a firm tone – let go and walk away from your dog.

• *Any time you reprimand your dog, it is important you balance his mental well being by praising him. Either praise your dog as soon as he stops doing the wrong action or in severe cases, ask him to do an action e.g., 'sit' or 'in bed' and praise him for doing this.*

The more negative you are when telling him off, the more positive you should be when he stops doing wrong, to balance him mentally. Otherwise, you could cause stress or anxiety.

3 YOUR NEW PUPPY/DOG

A dog's temperament is built on two factors:
- Heredity
- Experience

Which breed?

Deciding which breed you would like could be one of your most important decisions.

Over the centuries we have bred dogs and developed their individual traits to perform particular functions, for example: guarding, herding, hunting or being a house companion.

As we have heightened these natural instincts, the breed of dog you pick will possess these particular traits.

Take your time when choosing any puppy or dog, making sure you have a knowledge of the breed – meet as many of that particular breed as you can.

Talk to breeders, owners, vets, dog behaviourists and research suitability to your needs through books – there are plenty on the market about the different breeds of dogs.

Even when choosing a mongrel or cross breed, still consider the combination of the breed characteristics.

Questions to ask yourself:

What breed ?
- What has that particular breed been bred for?
- How compatible is the breed's character to your own and your family situation?

All dogs are individuals, but as a rough guide, for example:

Dobermans, German Shepherds, Rottweilers, Rhodesian Ridgebacks, Boxers will naturally guard and will have strong characters with dominant tendencies.

Border Collies, German Shepherds, Belgian Shepherds, Corgis, Bearded Collies will naturally herd and will be mentally alert.

Springer Spaniels, Setters, Pointers will naturally hunt and have excitable temperaments.

Labradors, Golden Retrievers, flat coated retrievers will naturally hunt and carry objects, but are relatively easy to train.

Any hounds will have an independent side when in an open environment.

Any terriers will have a strong character and tend to mouth and bark more than some other breeds.

What size?
You need to consider how big your puppy will grow.

- Is your chosen breed size suitable for the size of your house, garden and car?
- Is your chosen breed size suitable to live with young children?

Long or short haired ?
How much time to you have to devote to grooming?
Some long haired breeds will need to be groomed daily and
may require extra expenditure for clipping or professional
attention.

A dog or a bitch?
Dogs in general will have a stronger character.

How much time can I devote to exercise, mental stimulation?
The amount of physical exercise and mental simulation the dog
needs will vary from breed to breed.

Will the breed be suitable to live with children?
Consider size, as larger dogs can easily knock children over.
More dominant dogs will subtly dominate children.

*Is the breed suitable, taking into account my amount of
experience with dogs?*
Breeds vary greatly in suitability to train and adaptability to your
handling. Consider dominance levels, excitability, independence
levels, adaptability and initiative.

How many hours a day will the dog be left alone?
Dogs are pack animals and therefore are not mentally
designed to be on their own at all.
A dog can be left alone, with some consideration.
Four/five hours is acceptable once your dog is secure.
Mentally active, sensitive and excitable dogs may have more
 problems when left.

How much money can I afford?
Consider purchase price, vaccinations, vets' fees, insurance,
food, professional grooming.

You should pick a reputable breeder who shows concern for his dogs. If possible, ask to see both parents and any of the older generations in the family.

Make sure the dogs are relaxed and friendly; ask questions, as anyone who is honest will welcome your queries.

Make sure all the puppies look healthy and are active.

Do not buy a puppy because you feel sorry for it!

When viewing a litter, spend time with the puppies and observe their reactions to each other as well as how they react to you.

If you are inexperienced about dog-owning, have young children or lead a quiet lifestyle, picking the boldest, most outgoing puppy, which bounds up to you, may not be your best choice.

If you are quite outgoing or have a hectic lifestyle, picking the shy puppy in the corner could be a mistake.

Picking a 'middle of the road' puppy would be best if you are unsure.

Take someone with you who has a good knowledge of dogs.

Rescue and re-homed dogs

When buying an adult dog from a rescue home or a re-homing scheme, ask to spend some time with him to observe his reactions to different situations, people and other animals.

Again, ask as many questions as you can about how the dog has reacted since they have known him. As the history of his life may be unknown, you must deal with the present rather than being too preoccupied with his past.

As your dog only thinks for the moment and learns from associations, this is an ideal time for you to start afresh, educating and training him as you wish. Do not worry about what commands he may or may not know or what his previous name was. Start from the beginning, this way, you will avoid confusion.

A rescue dog may have bad associations with certain situations and old habits of behaviour. This again is an ideal time for re-education and reversal exercises. His confidence is likely to be low as he adapts to his new surroundings, so

making him feel secure with your company, as well as your home, will be a priority.

Subtle domination can be used from the beginning so you should start as you mean to go on.

Take your time when picking a rescue dog as you could end up with more problems than you bargained for. It is not fair on him to be taken back if you decide you cannot cope!

Introducing dogs

If you are buying a second dog, whether he is a puppy or an adult, the introduction is very important.

Your original dog may feel protective, under-confident or the need to jostle for your attention, as his home is being invaded by this new arrival.

If possible introduce the dogs initially on neutral territory, in an enclosed area outside. Try not to restrict them, as the more confined they feel, the more likely they are to be defensive or nervous. If you need to introduce them on leads, keep them as loose as possible.

Allow them to interact and settle in their own time; too much intervention from you can hinder them.

In a casual manner initially treat your original dog as number one, greeting him first and allowing him to continue with his old routines. Then gradually they will form their own relationship and you can treat them equally.

Picking up your puppy

When picking up your puppy, make sure you have your home ready for the new member of the family.

Advise visitors and children to be relaxed but friendly in the way they greet him initially, as, although he will be excited, he will also find the change in his surroundings quite stressful.

At this young age he will also need plenty of rest and time to be left alone.

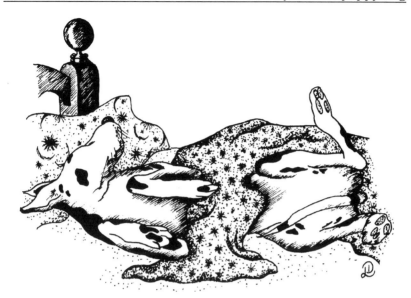

Sleeping arrangements

Choose an area where your puppy will sleep. *Start as you mean to go on* – don't have him sleeping in your bedroom if you want him eventually to sleep in the kitchen. The area should be warm and relatively small, as this will give your puppy security.

When collecting your puppy, take with you a towel or blanket and ask the breeder to rub this over the bitch and others in the litter. This familiar scent will give him a sense of security and lessen the worry of leaving his only known existence. Also take a cardboard box for your puppy to travel home in (with the towel or blanket inside). This box should then be used initially as his bed (cut the front out so he can get in and out) as he will have already felt this is his safe, secure place.

If your puppy is unsettled or distressed after leaving the other litter members, be confident and reassuring rather than over-supportive. Remember, you reinforce the behaviour your dog is showing at the time.

If the puppy is unsettled, have the cardboard box on your knee and talk and stroke the puppy whilst it is in there. If your puppy is feeling very under-confident and is allowed to physically cling to you, he will feel even more alone and deserted when you leave him for the first night.

It is likely that your puppy will cry or bark the first few nights when left alone as this will be the first time he has had no company. A hot water bottle wrapped in a blanket or a cuddly toy of some description can help him to settle, as well as the blanket with the litter mates' scent on it. (also see Problems when left – Chapter 5)

Do not go downstairs to your puppy when he is crying, as you will then teach him that when he cries you come, and you will cause an on-going problem.

Four to 12 weeks is the most impressionable time of your puppy's life.

Ideally you should pick up the puppy between 6 and 8 weeks old, this is a valuable time to start socialisation and habituation to your family and lifestyle.

By this time, he has spent valuable weeks with his litter mates and his mother learning the basics of canine communication.

Try to avoid traumatic experiences or bad associations at this time as they could have a lasting impression on your dog's temperament.

Feeding

Dogs will get a tremendous sense of security from routine, so keep feeding times regular.

If your puppy doesn't eat too well at first don't worry, as he may take time to adapt to his new environment. Don't leave food down all the time, as he will then learn he can pick at food whenever he wants and you will be discouraging him from eating well. Give your puppy five to ten minutes to eat then remove the bowl until the next feeding time as this will promote his natural protective instincts to eat when food is available.

Do not add any extra food to encourage your puppy to eat, because then he will learn a different lesson, that something more interesting will always come along.

Do not keep changing foods – pick a suitable food for the age of your dog and stick to it, otherwise you may encourage your puppy to be a fussy eater.

Naming

When choosing your puppy's name, pick something that suits his individuality.

Keep to simple names of one or two syllables so it is easy for him to learn.

Make sure that it sounds encouraging and positive as this will be your greatest tool for gaining your dog's attention in the future. Try to avoid names that sound like any common command you may use. Do not pick a name that you will find embarrassing to shout when out in the park!

To teach your puppy his name, simply use it any time you are getting his attention, when making a fuss of him and when feeding (or any positive activity).

House training

From day one, educate your puppy where you would like him to defecate and urinate (spend).

At this age he has not got the physical capacity to hold his motions for long, so formulate a routine to which he can get accustomed.

Regulate feeding times and give regular opportunity outside, in your required area, to spend.

Your puppy will usually need to spend soon after eating, when he has just woken up and when he has been running around or playing (exercise stimulates the bowels). At these times take your puppy outside and walk him around. If he spends in the required area, give him lots of praise as he is doing the action.

Accidents will happen as your puppy has no idea initially where he should and should not spend. Any time you catch him spending in an incorrect area, use a firm tone of voice, pick up your puppy or lead him to the doorway (before he actually spends or whilst doing so would be preferable to build the correct association), take him outside and praise if he continues in the appropriate place.

Your puppy will not be able to last the night without spending until roughly 14 weeks old, so before then, also whenever you leave him or cannot watch him, put him in his sleeping area (which should be reasonably confined – boarding a temporary area off or using a puppy crate in the beginning can help).

Initially cover the remaining area, other than his bed, with newspaper so when he does spend, it will be on the paper. Gradually reduce the area you cover as, if your puppy associates spending on the paper, he will continue to do so. Place the paper away from your dog's bed (as he will not defecate near this area) and towards the door you wish him to exit through.

With consistent reinforcement and by telling your puppy off only if you catch him in the act, he will quickly learn to spend outside.

If you have children or value your lawn, teach your puppy to spend in a particular area in your garden by simply taking him to the spot when you're reinforcing his routines.

TEMPERAMENT-BUILDING EXERCISES

Every puppy has his own individual temperament and character. From an early age it is important to do some simple exercises to help build an adaptable, friendly dog.

Habituation and socialisation

As mentioned earlier, 4 to 12 weeks is the most impressionable time of your dog's life.

Start as you mean to go on. At home, formulate your routines, subject your dog to any situation (in a controlled manner) that you would like him to cope with in the future. Once you have your puppy, book him in with your local vet for his required vaccinations, which will be given over a period of a few weeks. Until your puppy's vaccinations are complete do not take him to any area where he could be at risk of infection. You can take your puppy and introduce him to the outside world, but only if you are able to carry him.

Your puppy should:

- Come into contact with women, men and children
- Come into contact with other animals
- Play, off the lead, with other dogs

- Be left with other people
- Be left alone
- Travel in the car
- Be subject to crowds and traffic

You should not throw your puppy in the deep end but gradually introduce different aspects, depending on how he is coping with his new life. The younger the dog, the more adaptable his nature, so try to develop this as early on as possible.

Remember, your attitude is important as this will be transmitted to your puppy: be confident and relaxed in these situations. Never force your puppy to make friends with anyone – let him dictate the pace. If he is worried or frightened, give him some space away from the stimulus, get him to sit and just allow him to watch the situation, reassure him when he relaxes.

Your puppy already has some dog socialisation experience from his litter mates and mother but it is only an introduction and now it is very important that you take time to develop and continue this.

Socialisation with other dogs off the lead is important, as, with lead restriction, he will react in a more defensive manner; he will feel unable to escape if he needs to. Socialisation on the lead could be detrimental for nervous or under-confident dogs.

Try not to be too over-protective of your puppy when he is playing with other dogs – biting and play fighting are all important games he will want to play whilst learning valuable interaction.

Handling

Physical interaction with all the family is very important – using play and gentle affection. Also get him used to having his ears, eyes, mouth, body, tail and feet handled – get family and friends to do the same. If he is worried or fidgety use food to distract him so he can get used to this contact. This is particularly important to gradually habituate your puppy for future handling, whether visiting the vet, groomers or having his nails clipped.

Picking your dog up can also help him to get used to physical contact from others – make sure you hold him with one arm under his chest and the other around his back legs so you give ample support and keep his spine as straight as possible.

Grabbing

Over a period of time your puppy can become sensitive about you or strangers grabbing or touching him when he isn't expecting it; this is usually associated with being told off.

Exercises can be beneficial to reverse this – regularly grab your dog as it passes you or when it is unsuspecting. As you grab him, have some food in the other hand, therefore he learns it is positive to be grabbed. When he is happy with you doing this, ask your visitors to do the same. Again, this is a valuable exercise as you may need your dog to be grabbed by strangers in the future (e.g. if he escapes).

Settling when excitable

Teaching your dog to settle in excitable situations is important from a young age, as, remember, he will learn from habit and association.

Puppies find many aspects of life very exciting and over a period of time they end up having an inability to switch off and relax.

Teach your puppy to entertain himself in such situations by giving him a bone, a chew or something he can play with himself (only allow him to have this when you want him to, take it away once your visitors have left).

Teach him to go into his bed on command, even if you move his bed from room to room, so he can still benefit from your companionship.

GENERAL EDUCATION

Remember how your puppy thinks: he will only learn from association. Tell him something is wrong while he is doing it, then praise him as soon as he stops.

Praise your pupppy for good behaviour even if you haven't asked him to do the action as this will encourage him to repeat it.

Chewing articles

When your puppy is chewing something inappropriate tell him it is incorrect; then replace the article with something that is acceptable, then praise him for chewing that article.

As chewing is an essential activity for jaw and teeth development so appropriate toys should be left with him at all times.

Mouthing (see Chapter 5)
Jumping Up (see Chapter 5)
Attention Seeking (see Chapter 5)

Your puppy and children

As dogs are pack animals, your children are usually victims of subtle domination from your puppy, as they are the physically shorter and mentally the weakest members of the family.

Therefore, all members of the family should interact with him and subtly dominate him in the same way whenever possible. Heavy control by adult members of the family will undermine your children's position.

> • *Teach your children simple obedience sessions (see Chapter 3) as this will not only educate your dog, but will help them to control him.*
> • *Mouthing and jumping up exercises should also be carried out whenever possible.(see Chapter 5)*
> • *A simple exercise to teach children is to use their body posture. When your puppy is over-excitable towards them, they should stand up quickly. This is a subtle form of domination.*

> • *On a regular basis teach your child to stand upright, with an arm outstretched, holding a biscuit – they can then feed your puppy when he sits in front of them (you may need to help them initially by holding your puppy to stop him jumping up). If this is repeated several times a day, your puppy will soon associate that at any time your child does this action he automatically sits. Then whenever your child is having a problem in calming down the puppy, teach him or her to carry out this routine.*

NEUTERING YOUR PUPPY

Castration

Considering your puppy's temperament, the best time to castrate him is as soon as he starts to cock his leg. He will naturally cock his leg as his hormones start to increase, on an average at eight months old. Do not try and teach your puppy this action, as it will be a natural process as he develops.

For a well behaved, socially acceptable dog, castration is advised and this process, although it sounds severe, is a relatively minor operation, which has so many temperamental and training benefits.

If your puppy is left uncastrated it could:

• Be prone to straying from your home
• Have hormone fluctuations which may be bought on through any excitable situations (e.g. excessive excitability or mounting)
• Be more likely to question your authority
• Have a stronger 'doggy' odour
• Urinate / mark by cocking his leg, even in your home or any new environment.

Having your puppy castrated as soon as he starts cocking his leg will prevent any hormonal influences affecting your dog's temperament; this will NOT affect his individuality.

• *Do not wait for problems to occur.*

If you decide to castrate later due to problems you are experiencing, you will not gain any ground lost, only halt the puppy hormonally at that time.

Castration will naturally slow your puppy's metabolic rate, therefore a small reduction in his food may be required to compensate.

A dog's hormonal level will increase up to the age of four, and fluctuates throughout his life. Hormones affect dogs'

behaviour not their fundamental characters, so castration will not change your dog's personality, but will make him more biddable, avoid sexual frustration and help him to lead a more happy and balanced existence.

Spaying

A bitch will have her first season from seven months to one year old. Before this time you will probably see hormone fluctuations where she is more excitable or more sensitive and quiet which could occur even a month before her first season.

Your dog's season will last approximately three weeks; in this time she is vulnerable to mating, with the second week the time she is receptive. Changes in her temperament can occur before, during and after her season.

The ideal time to spay a bitch is in mid-cycle after her first season and your local veterinary practice should be contacted to decide the preferable dates.

Due to your dog's mentality, it makes no difference to her whether she is allowed to conceive a litter of puppies or not.

4 OBEDIENCE

For puppies or any newly acquired adult dog, teaching and educating him so your commands are fully understood is important before you can expect him to respond to you in different situations.

Suggested commands

Stand
Sit
Down
Upsit
Stay
Come

Choose the commands you would like to use and start by building a word association with the particular action. *If you ask your dog to sit three times he will quickly learn he does not have to sit on the first command.*

Initially, until you are sure your dog understands, say the command as he does the action, so he learns by word association. (For a quick reference, see the table on page 27).

Keep all exercises short and positive so your dog enjoys himself; this will aid learning. Try to avoid your dog becoming bored with what you are trying to teach him and always end exercises on a positive note.

The use of food or a favourite toy can assist you when trying to teach your dog a new command at any stage of his life. Do not look at this as a defeatist way of training him, as it is a valuable tool to promote concentration if there are other distractions.

If you give food as a reward, do this randomly, so your dog will not automatically expect it; otherwise he will start to weigh up whether the bribe is worth his while! Food can be used in your hand to keep his concentration but you do not have to always feed him with it.

Food should be used in conjunction with vocal command and praise. Do not overfeed your dog; try using part of his normal diet, as this will avoid unnecessary weight gain.

Stand

Stand can be an important position to teach your dog and can be used for a variety of control situations such as grooming, clipping, bathing and veterinary examinations.

> • *Use food in your hand to gain the dog's concentration and position it on the end of his nose.*
> • *Draw your hand out horizontally in front of you, not the dog, until he stands to follow it, then reinforce vocally with 'Good boy to stand' as he carries out the action.*
> • *Physically reinforce by slowly stroking the dog with the other hand. Quite often a pressure point on the dog's hindquarters or back, if scratched or pushed, can encourage the dog to push back towards your hand, therefore reinforcing his position.*

Sit

Sit can be used as a valuable control method for any situation and should be regarded as a temporary position.

> • *From a stand, bring your hand backwards slowly over the dog's head; if the dog's head comes up, his bottom naturally goes down.*
> • *Say the command 'Good boy to sit' as the dog does the action. Stroking can be used to physically reinforce.*

Down

Down is a valuable and effective control position for different situations, but used effectively will also encourage your dog to settle and relax.

Remember, the smaller a dog makes itself, the more submissive it is being, therefore by teaching your dog to willingly lie down on command, is in effect to dominate him.

- *From a sit or a stand place your hand on the floor in front of his paws with the food underneath your hand.*
- *By doing this, the dog has to lie down to reach it.*
- *In many cases this will be the hardest position for you to achieve initially with your dog, so to increase his willingness, simply feed as soon as he lies down if required. Reinforce vocally 'Good boy down' as he is doing the action.*
- *Physically stroking your dog in a slow reassuring manner will reinforce this position.*

Upsit

Use upsit as an intermediate command when finishing a 'Down' to build an association that the dog does not leap straight up from that position.

• From a 'Down' position slowly raise your hand vertically with the food to encourage your dog into a 'sit' position.
• A positive vocal command 'Upsit' as the dog does the action will reinforce your command.

Stay

Stay can be used to reinforce a 'Sit' or 'Down' command.

With puppies or young dogs, develop the 'down' stay and keep a 'sit' stay as a temporary position for short sessions (as the muscles on your dog do not develop fully until approximately a year old, prolonged sit stays should be avoided until this time).

• Simply hold the position you require your dog to stay in and reinforce vocally with, 'Good boy to stay' by keeping your hand with the food stable, reassuring physical praise will help you to reinforce this.

Come

Come is a valuable command to reinforce from an early age.

• Walk backwards using food and a positive body posture reinforcing vocally, 'Good boy to come' as your dog walks towards you.
• At any time you call your dog in the house or garden, first consider your body posture, bend down and vocally sound encouraging to your dog.
• Only call your dog once and if he ignores this, walk towards him, put your hand with the food in it towards his nose, then walk backwards repeating, 'Good boy to come' therefore reinforcing what was required in the first place.

Practise simple obedience exercises prior to feeding your dog his meal, when putting his lead on, or any activity with positive associations; this will greatly accelerate his willingness to learn.

All members of your family – including children – should practise obedience in different situations with your dog as this will help form a pattern of behaviour and make sure that they too are in control.

DEVELOPMENT

Once you are sure your dog has a clear understanding of what is meant by each command, gradually increase the time spent on these exercises as his concentration improves.

Introduce distractions: for example, set up situations with family or friends, by getting them to try and distract your dog. Whilst you are practising obedience, vary your expectations according to the environment your dog is in. (e.g. he is more likely to concentrate when in the house than in the park).

Gradually reduce the use of food when there are no distractions, but still use food if necessary when your dog's concentration is likely to waver.

Even when you have stopped using food, still place your hand in the same position as when using it. This will aid your dog's understanding of what is required; for example, when asking your dog to sit, bring your hand up and when asking him to go down, point to the floor.

> • *Only ask your dog to do the action once – the second time you must make sure he completes it.*
> • *When commanding your dog to undertake an action, praise if successful.*
> • *If your dog ignores you, you must reinforce what was required otherwise he will quickly learn he does not have to do it for you. Reinforcement can either be a firmer vocal command the second time or physically guiding the dog with your hand into that position.*

Stand

• Physically reinforce by gently pushing or stroking on his hindquarters or sides. Gently lift the dog into stand position by placing a hand under his ribcage.

Sit

• Push your dog's hindquarters down into his front legs.

Down

• *Gently push down from behind your dog's shoulder blades.*

Upsit

• *Either slowly slide your foot under his chest or step backwards to encourage the upsit position.*

Stay

Gradually increase the amount of distance between you and your dog. Start by being able to stand up and bend down next to your dog without him moving, reinforcing the vocal command frequently to keep his concentration.

- *Circle slowly around the front of your dog, increasing the size of the radius and eventually walk around him.*
- *Regularly reinforce in close proximity; for example, bending down three foot away from your dog without him moving or touching him; going back and stroking him, then leaving again.*
- *Set up situations of other distractions while you are standing next to him. This will be a lot more beneficial in reinforcing your dog's understanding of stay, rather than immediately leaving him and trying to reinforce from a distance.*
- *Gradually remove the use of food on the stay exercises so your dog is not focusing on your hand and concentrating more on the vocal command and body posture.*

Reinforcement

Over a period of time gradually reinforce all aspects of obedience with your dog, varying duration and environment.

Gradually drop off the use of food and toys, but they can be used in the future as positive attention-gainers at high incentive times.

Always reinforce your dog's response in an appropriate way and consider there will always be times his behaviour is not perfect.

LEADWORK
Introduction of the collar and lead

Pick a suitable puppy collar and lead, do not use a check chain until your puppy is over a year old as physical damage can be inflicted due to his bones not sufficiently calcifying until this time.

Your puppy may find the new sensation of a collar around his neck quite strange so initially build a positive association by putting on the collar for small sessions during feeding time and physical affection. After a few days, leave the collar on full time – make sure it is fitted correctly, with enough room beneath it to fit two or three fingers.

Fitting the lead should be carried out again initially in short positive sessions and you should avoid jerking or pulling your puppy around. Use food or a toy to distract your puppy so he gets used to walking along with the lead on. Members of the family can help by calling him.

Developing controlled leadwork

Your dog is likely to go through a stage of pulling on the lead – in any direction.

The whole theory of successful leadwork is to build an association with your dog, not to absorb any tension through the lead – it takes two to pull, you should also practise not pulling against him and aim to have the lead slack at all times.

Whenever you have your dog on a lead, whether you are putting your shoes or coat on, opening your car or out for a walk, *never hold your dog physically in any position by use of the lead*. At times when you are both stationary, ask your dog to sit, stand or stay so he doesn't pull.

Formulate obedience routines when putting on the lead, getting ready for a walk. When leaving the front door and gate and getting in and out of the car, get your dog to sit/stay at doors using vocal commands. Call him through once you are ready. The more you can calm and control your dog in these situations, the more he will listen to you once you are out in the open.

Decide which side you would prefer your dog to walk; this can vary, but you should decide to change, not your dog.

While walking, if you regularly let your dog off the lead, there is no need for him to be dragging you around to sniff.

Make him walk next to you, as he will learn to dominate through taking you where he wants to go; he will also be less likely to come back when he is off the lead if you have relied too much on physical restriction to control him.

When he is free, he will have all the time in the world to be a dog.

• Hold your lead in a relaxed manner in your hand, allowing enough slack so you are not creating the tension, otherwise you will be encouraging your dog to pull.

• If he pulls into the lead, flick the lead back in a quick sharp manner. It is the quickness of the action that the dog responds to, not the physical strength. (You will not hurt your dog by doing this – more long-term damage will be done by continually pulling.)

• *Do not absorb any tension – as your dog only learns from associations, make the association between tension and unacceptability very clear. If you absorb some tension and then correct your dog he will not understand; your inconsistency will be confusing.*
• *Couple your jerk action with a command such as 'Heel' or 'Steady'.*
• *After a period of time, use your vocal command first, then, if your dog ignores it, pull back on the lead repeating the vocal command. This will improve his voice response.*
• *Always vocally praise your dog when the correct position or 'lack of' tension is achieved.*
• *Try not to worry too much initially if the dog is not exactly at heel as the association of no tension is your priority to establish.*

Use extra reinforcers such as:

• *Calling your dog back to your side as you walk backwards – pause for a moment, slapping your side with 'Good boy to heel', then resuming your original direction will help to make your wishes clear.*
• *Asking your dog to sit-come-sit-come in an exciting positive manner will help you to gain some concentration and also subtly dominate him if he is distracted or not listening to you.*
• *Suddenly changing direction, especially at high incentive times; for example, just before you are about to enter the park, to make your dog realise he has to follow you not the other way round.*
• *Food or toys can be used in your hand to gain and keep your dog's attention for a while to allow you to build a positive word association with the command.*
• *If your dog is attempting to chase cars or joggers or becoming over-excited when meeting people whilst he is on the lead, the same procedure should be used.*
• *If your dog is too excited, ask him to sit and stay while the distraction passes then resume your walk.*

Off-lead heelwork

Training your dog to walk to heel without a lead can be a valuable training aid to improve your vocal control. When your dog is free, calling him back to heel when you're nearing a distraction such as other dogs on leads, a family with small children, or when passing other animals is a vital tool.

Using your vocal command in this way will also help improve your leadwork. When we use a lead, we tend to rely too much on the physical restriction for control situations. Because of this, the dog is not listening to your vocal commands.

However well trained your dog is at off the lead control, you should remember it is a legal requirement for your dog to be on a lead on a public highway, some designated footpaths and when livestock is present.

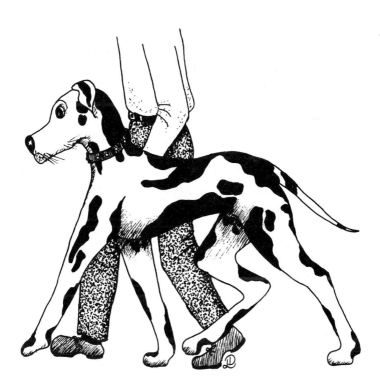

Because of your dog's mental reasoning ability, he will not recognise that a car is a serious danger. Your dog may be distracted or scared by something, which could quite easily cause him to run out in front of a vehicle. If this happens, you will also be liable for the accident caused by your dog.

Off the lead heelwork can be introduced at any age.

• *Use food or a toy initially to keep your dog's concentration. Choose which side you would like him to be; this can change but only if you allow it!*

• *Face the direction you are going to be walking – ask your dog to sit and gain his concentration before removing the lead*

• *Hold your hand, with food or a toy, next to your side in the position where your require your dog to walk. Slap your leg and use vocal commands 'Heel' or 'Steady' as you start to move*

• *Praise your dog when he is in the correct position*

• *With off-lead heelwork the association you build with your dog needs to be quite clear – as soon as he moves too far ahead or wide of you, repeat your command in a firmer negative tone*

• *Praise when his correct position is resumed*

• *You may need to use extra reinforcers such as the 'Sit' command at regular intervals as this will help keep his concentration and stop him dashing ahead*

• *If you have to use your negative vocal command, suddenly walk backwards, slapping your side to encourage your dog back towards you. As he comes next to you, then move forwards again to resume the correct position. Repeat this at any time during the exercise, especially when he is too far ahead. Try to build an association of what is required*

• *Practise sessions with quick 90° turns and vary your speed. This will also help to reinforce your vocal command*

• *Initially, make sure you always command your dog to sit before letting him run free*

• *Start with short sessions of approximately ten paces and gradually build up the distance to increase your dog's heel and concentration abilities*

• *Remember, start to educate your dog in a distraction-free environment, for example at home. Once you are confident, build your dog's response with other distractions present*

• *Reduce the use of food or a toy so your dog is responding to your vocal command and praise*

RECALLING YOUR DOG

Dogs are pack animals so they will naturally stay in close proximity to the pack leader, who of course is you.

Your dog's recall can break down over a period of time if you habitually follow him wherever he goes.

If you call your dog repeatedly and he ignores you, this gives him the message that he doesn't have to come back.

Releasing your dog in an open environment

- *Practise 'Come' at home in a controlled environment or initially on a long lead. Use an encouraging body posture, vocal command and any excitable action such as clapping. This will help to make you more inviting. Reinforce effectively and praise if your dog responds.*
- *Choose a safe environment, which is relatively enclosed and away from public highways.*
- *Initially, choose a quiet time so you gain confidence with your dog and have time to reinforce the 'Come' response with minimal distractions.*

• *You should let your dog off in an open environment from an early age, as at this time your puppy lacks confidence in the environment and will naturally stick close to you. This will enable you to reinforce his recall in an instinctive way and save yourself training time.*
• *Practise some simple obedience prior to releasing him – preferably off the lead – to build his concentration on you and to subtly dominate him.*

As mentioned earlier, dogs are pack animals and will therefore naturally follow the pack – this is your key to good recall.

Always

• *Regularly hide and change direction without telling your dog. Set yourself a mental radius; if your dog goes out of this, walk in the opposite direction in a positive manner. Actively*

try to panic him, in a controlled situation, by hiding behind a tree or bush.
• Vary your walks and routes – become unpredictable.
• When meeting other people or dogs, condition him to naturally follow you by just walking away rather than collecting him first. This will heighten his natural pack instincts and make him more dependent on you in an open environment.

If you always call your dog or let him know when you are changing direction, he will learn not to concentrate on you until you call his name.

If you have an older dog with a recall problem, try walking him in unknown areas initially while you build up his concentration level.

If your dog naturally follows you, it will lessen the necessity of keeping calling, as, wherever you go, whatever you do, he will be with you.

When calling your dog

• Call your dog only once with your voice or a whistle. Remember to maintain an encouraging body posture and use physical gestures.
• Praise him when he returns.

If you call your dog six times he will quickly learn he can return in his own time and when he feels like it.

If your dog ignores you, reinforce his recall effectively – always practise one or a combination of the following, as your dog will learn from each experience:

• *Walk off and hide without calling again*
• *Use a negative tone of voice or throw something next to your dog to gain his attention; as soon as he looks at you, call in a positive way.*

If you do not balance the negativity by positively calling your dog once his attention has been gained, you will discourage him from returning. Never tell your dog off if he returns, however long it has taken, as he will then associate that coming back is wrong, rather than what he was doing before he came back.

> • *Go to your dog without calling again. Catch your dog or use food to get his attention, then walk backwards reinforcing 'Good boy to come.'*
> • *If using a whistle to recall your dog, build a positive association with the whistle in your home, as then it will be more likely to gain his attention in an open environment and when he is distracted.*
> • *Ask your dog to sit and stay for his meal or for any positive incentive, such as a toy. Blow the whistle as an indicator that he can now claim his prize.*
> • *To begin with, he will have no association for the whistle, so use physical signs to reinforce the action, gradually reducing these until the whistle acts as the sole indicator.*

5 COMMON PROBLEMS

Jumping up

Jumping up is a common trait in a majority of dogs, a habit which forms from excitablity when greeting you and others or when demanding attention.

Your dog jumps up in innocence, but, unless controlled, he will inadvertently learn to dominate you as he is making himself bigger when lungeing towards you.

If you allow your dog to jump up, he will also do the same to visitors or unsuspecting walkers in the park.

This is a dominance-based trait, you will improve your overall control by solving this problem.

This method should also be used when your dog is giving you or others unwanted physical attention or in cases when he is mounting people in a sexual manner.

• *The most important thing to remember is body posture. You must remain upright, as bending down to stroke your dog or push him away will show submission in your body posture (inadvertently reinforcing your dog's behaviour).*
• *Remember to use eye contact when you push your dog off.*
• *Quickly raise your knee, making contact with the dog. Don't worry, you won't hurt him, dogs are very physically resilient (at least four times more so than humans).*
• *When kneeing your dog away, always use a command, for example 'Off' in a firm tone. This will build the correct association that the jumping up is wrong, not the greeting. Once he has backed down, you must praise him vocally as soon as he has all four paws on the ground – therefore, he will associate it's the jumping up that is wrong, not that you are displeased to see him.*

Stand upright
Look at your dog
Knee off
Command: 'Off'
Vocally praise when achieved

• *Even if you are sitting down, follow the same procedure, but push the dog away with your hand. If he persists, stand up to bring dominance into your body posture.*

Mouthing

Mouthing is a natural and essential behaviour for your dog – it promotes jaw and teeth development – but there are plenty of other good chewing implements other than you!

Dogs mouth in play, but this is still a dominance-based game. By stopping him mouthing, you will gain more respect and give him a conscience not to put his mouth on you or others.

Over time, you will also heighten your dog's bite inhibition, so if he does unfortunately bite, the severity of the bite will be less. He will have learnt that humans are delicate, so excessive force or multiple bites are not necessary. If your dog mouths in play, he will be more likely to bite in a fear or protective situation.

If you see two dogs playing, they play very roughly with their mouths, but they will not draw blood or break the skin.

If one dog cries as it is hurt, the game will stop, even if momentarily and this will indicate to the other dog that the play was a little too hard. The game will then resume, the parameters as to how hard they can play now having been set.

*Following the same principle, you need to tell your dog that **ANY** tooth contact hurts, therefore over a period of time this will help soften the dog's mouth contact and eliminate mouthing.*

Tell your dog that mouth contact with hair, clothes, even shoes will hurt, so that he will associate that these objects are attached to you.

Hand feeding your dog will greatly accelerate the process. Feed his dinner and small titbits placed between your fingers, again telling your dog it hurts and withdrawing the food until he takes it without touching you with his teeth.

Command: 'Ouch' at any time your dog touches you with his teeth.

When sitting down, or when you or small children are playing on the floor with your dog, it may be necessary to stand up suddenly when saying 'Ouch,' to bring dominance into your body posture.

Jumping on furniture

It is acceptable for your dog to sleep on the furniture, but only if you allow it. The decision should be yours, not his.

If you want your dog on the sofa for a cuddle, or like him sleeping at the foot of the bed, this is not a problem. However, you could be encouraging a conflict, so make sure you invite him on and off as you wish.

You need to be able to tell him when to get off when required.

If your dog is not allowed on the furniture and only indulges in this pleasure when you are not present, this could indicate insecurity when your dog is left (see Problems when left, p. 92).

> • *From an early age, your dog should be made aware of whether he is allowed on the furniture or not. If not, when he gets on the furniture, or appears to have the intention, use a vocal command such as 'Off' in a firm tone coupled with a hand gesture pointing to the floor. If your dog ignores this, then:*
> • *For puppies or dogs that need education, it is important to reinforce a positive association with the command. Therefore, a treat or biscuit thrown on the floor next to the furniture can be used to encourage your dog off after the initial command. Vocally praise when he jumps down to get the reward.*

• *If you're sure your dog has a clear understanding that he should not be on the furniture, vocally command him 'Off', again using hand gestures. If disobeyed, reinforce the command by sharply pulling either the cushion or the duvet out from underneath him, pulling him to the ground. It is not a good idea always to physically grab your dog, as, for stubborn breeds, this will encourage him to fight against you. Always praise your dog once the action is complete.*

• *If you like your dog on the furniture, it is a good idea to build an association with a particular stimulus, for example: teach your dog that a rug or a towel placed on the furniture is a sign he can get on. This will make it clear in his mind.*

• *It is still important to practise telling your dog he has to get off the furniture on command as this will subtly dominate and avoid him becoming protective.*

• *For dogs sleeping on the furniture when the owner is not present, (See Problems when left section) set up situations where you dash back into the room and catch your dog on the furniture following either one of the steps above.*

• *Dogs only learn through association and habit, so by placing, for example, silver foil or coat hangers on the furniture, you will discourage him from getting on and help to prevent the action. This is a good technique to use if you are not present to reinforce this yourself.*

Excitability with visitors

An over-excitable dog when visitors arrive in the house can become anti-social and embarrassing. Unfortunately, not everyone is a dog lover!

It's ironic, though, that it's the visitors that cause the problem with your dog in the first place. When you have a puppy, he has learnt that he is the centre of attention when people enter the house.

A dog barking, jumping up or fussing around for attention needs to be controlled.

• *To reverse the association that everyone coming into the house wants attention from your dog, encourage your visitors to adopt a casual attitude and just vocally praise him when entering the house.*

When they have been in the house for a period of time, they can then approach your dog on their terms, playing or interacting with him as they wish. It's your responsibility to control the initial barking (see Barking) and jumping up.

• *It may help you to keep a slip lead by your door and put it on your dog, asking him to sit before you open the door. Do not physically restrain him, but if he leaps towards your visitors, pull the lead back firmly using the command 'Off', so he associates he should not jump up. When answering the door or greeting people, you should have your dog sitting next to you or behind you, as you are then physically putting yourself in a control position.*

• *If you have visitors, give your dog a bone or chew at this time to encourage him to entertain himself (removing the toy once they have left). If control is needed, vocally command your dog (see Jumping Up) or use obedience or 'In-bed' commands to tell him what is required.*

• *Often in these situations a dog becomes excitable simply because it does not know what else to do, therefore it is up to you to tell him what is required.*

• *Always praise him vocally when he has settled.*

Attention-seeking

Dogs can and will seek attention 24 hours a day. This is a dominance-based activity, as your dog is demanding affection, games or attention on his terms.

Attention-seeking problems can manifest themselves when you are concentrating on something that does not involve your dog. For example, with visitors, watching the television, physical interaction with your family, or when you are speaking on the telephone.

This method can also be used at meal times if your dog is begging for food.

• Try to formulate subtle routines when visitors arrive at the house. For example, give your dog a bone, chew or a mentally stimulating toy, so that he will learn to entertain himself at these times. This item should be removed at all other times, so your dog does not become bored with it.
• From an early age on a casual basis, all affection, games and attention should be on your terms, not his.
• If your dog regularly attention-seeks, use the vocal command 'Off' and praise him when he has walked away

from you (vocal praise rather than physical is more appropriate as it is the physical attention your dog was seeking in the first place).
• Remember, reinforce good behaviour, e.g. if your dog is entertaining himself or goes and lies down, vocally praise him so he learns that is right.
• After 5 or 10 minutes, you can call your dog back and give him the affection or a game that is now on your terms.

Extra reinforcement may be needed at times like this as dogs are like children: any attention, positive or negative, is better than none at all. You can use a water spray, as the shock of the water hitting him in the face will make him more likely to listen to your command. This should only be used once you are sure he has an understanding of the vocal command.

• Always give your dog a location where you would like him to be, for instance, 'In your bed'.
• Ask him to go to his bed; if he ignores you take him there and put him on his bed, then praise. In very excitable situations he may keep trying to get off, keep reinforcing the command and use a negative command if he gets off, then balance with praise when he eventually settles down.

His bed can be moved from room to room to help him to settle in different situations.

If you are consistent, he will quickly learn in these situations to go to his bed; continue to reinforce with vocal praise.

Stealing items

A dog will steal items for a variety of different reasons, for example, lack of education about what is his and what is not, attention-seeking, or scavenging.

> • *To educate puppies or young dogs, it is important to build the right association about which possessions they can play with and which they cannot.*
> • *If your dog picks up an article you do not wish him to have, use a vocal command such as 'Leave it' and replace the item with something that is his or that is acceptable. Always praise your dog to reinforce which is the correct item to chew or play with.*
> • *If he regularly steals items such as cushions, tea-towels, etc., to gain attention from yourself or visitors, it is important not to enter a chase to retrieve the item, as this will only encourage the behaviour.*
> • *Try ignoring your dog, but obviously this may not always be appropriate. Vocally command him to 'Leave it' in a firm tone so your dog understands what he has is unacceptable. Praise him if he drops the item.*
> • *Throw something noisy, for example a bunch of keys, next to your dog to shock him, using a vocal command, then call him to you in a positive manner.*
> • *The problem with stealing food items is that your dog gains his own reward each time. Food surfaces should be cleared away if you are not present to control this problem. At other times, regularly set up situations where you are leaving food readily available for him to steal. Either vocally command your dog to 'Leave it' in a sharp tone or, again, throw something next to him to shock him as he attempts to steal the item. Praise if successful.*

Gradually progress exercises to enable more distance between you and the food, eventually leaving the room for short periods, but being prepared to dash back in to control your dog if necessary.

If your dog steals items when you are out but not when you are at home, he will be feeling insecure, causing him to be too mentally alert – see problems when left.

Dropping items

Dogs are protective by nature, which can cause a reluctance to drop an item. It is also a dominance-based activity and it is advisable to teach the your dog to drop on command.

It will be a battle of strength, for example, if you pull an item from your dog's mouth or force the mouth open; in the majority of cases, this will encourage him to hang on tighter or even defend his possession by growling or biting.

• Teach your dog the vocal commands 'Leave it' or 'Drop'. Initially, it is important to build a positive association with leaving an article to reverse any protective tendencies in the dog.
• Place your hand on the article and a titbit on the dog's nose. As the dog releases his mouth, reinforce with a vocal command such as 'Good boy to leave'.
• Over a period of time, reduce the use of food and substitute vocal praise, this will build a positive association with the dog leaving / dropping an item – he has learnt that he will always get something better in return.
* If you are sure your dog understands 'Leave it' or 'Drop', reinforcement such as throwing something noisy next to the dog, coupled with your vocal command, will be more effective than physically confronting him. Always praise when achieved.

Problems when left

As dogs are pack animals, they are not mentally designed to be on their own. They will often get security out of your physical presence more than their surroundings. Any behaviour that a dog displays only when left alone is actually insecurity or panic.

A dog only thinks for the moment, so when he is left he will feel deserted. The three main danger times are: when your dog is initially left, if something disturbs him later on, or when you are expected home, as these are the times he will be most mentally active. You will usually find behaviour such as barking, destructiveness or inappropriate defecation will occur at these times.

Although over a period of time this type of behaviour can become a habit if your dog is left for long periods, it can also be associated with boredom.

It is important to increase your dog's own mental security or promote confidence in his environment.

* *Try to discourage your dog from following you around the house or from room to room. Use 'In bed' command or close doors behind you initially.*
* *Your attitude when leaving your dog and returning home is important. Act in a casual manner with vocal praise, as over-exciting him or too much physical contact will make your absence even more profound. When returning home, the more fuss you make, the more insecure you make your dog when he is left.*
* *Confine the area you leave him in, as the larger the area, the more insecure he will feel, as he will need to keep mentally aware for self-preservation.*
* *Shutting your dog in one room, preferably towards the back of the house, will lessen outside distractions and cause less stress. Even leaving your dog's bed under a table or in a confined area in the kitchen can promote a feeling of security. In severe cases of panic a dog crate can be used as this will help him to settle; feed him in there initially to build a positive association.*
* *A radio left on for background noise can help muffle any environmental sounds and give your dog a sense of companionship.*
* *A dog receives a tremendous sense of security from your smell, which is why he will sometimes steal dirty underwear, retreat to his owner's regular chair or bed, or sit on the driver's seat of the car. It is therefore a good substitute to make your dog a snuggle blanket.*
* *Use an old towel or sweatshirt to make a good snuggle blanket. Rub it over yourself before you have a bath so it has a very strong scent of you on it. Re-scent the blanket a couple of times a week and place it in your dog's bed.*

• Bones, chews or mentally stimulating toys should also be used at these times. If your dog is very insecure, you will find he will only want to eat these articles on your return, so it is important that you remove them as you come home. Then your dog will learn he has to eat them when he has the opportunity, therefore encouraging him to entertain himself if he is feeling mentally alert.

DO NOT TELL YOUR DOG OFF WHEN YOU RETURN HOME IF YOU FIND HE HAS DONE WRONG (UNLESS YOU CATCH HIM IN THE ACT), AS THIS WILL ONLY EXAGGERATE HIS INSECURITY AND IS LIKELY TO MAKE THE PROBLEM WORSE.

Barking

Barking is a common problem in all dogs. They will bark for a variety of reasons – attention seeking (see Attention-Seeking), when left (see When Left), protection of themselves, their territory or other pack members, apprehension and warning others away when under-confident or frightened.

Under the pack hierarchy the lower ranking members of the pack, such as your dog, will act as an early warning system to alert the others of danger. The higher ranking pack members, such as yourself, will then step in and take control.

Your puppy will not initially bark when people come into your house, as you are the protector at this early age. Once a dog hormonally matures, he will start to take a protective role in the pack. It is important, therefore, especially with guarding breeds, not to encourage your dog to bark, as he will naturally develop this trait.

• Teach your dog the understanding of the word 'Quiet'. You need to make it clear that the command is directed towards him as just by shouting, you will appear to be joining in with the behaviour and the whole pack is doing it together. Firm vocal command 'Quiet', followed with a 'Sit', will subtly dominate your dog.
• Using something to distract your dog – for example, some food or a toy – can help you to gain his concentration and quieten him; this will enable you to positively reinforce 'Good boy quiet'. Be careful not to feed him when he is still barking as this will only reinforce the behaviour.

Protective barking

If your dog is barking in a protective role, it is important you take control of the situation.

• Whether in the house or outside, the use of a lead can be helpful. Allow your dog to bark once or twice when someone comes to the door, then quieten vocally as above.
Remember, have your dog sitting next to you or behind you when answering the door as this will make it clear to the dog that you are in a control position.

Don't worry that by stopping your dog barking in these situations you will stop him being a good watchdog; you will not stop him defending you or your property when you are not present, or in a fear situation when you are scared: the dog will then resume the control role.

If your dog at any stage is protective of any members of the family it is important that all members interact with him in a similar manner; subtle domination should be used to show him his place in your pack hierarchy

Apprehensive barking

If your dog is nervous or unsure of a situation, he may bark as a warning and a self-defence mechanism.

> • *It is important in these situations to assume a confident and firm attitude, as above. If you are reassuring your dog, you will only reinforce the behaviour he is displaying, for example 'Good boy to bark'. Remember, show reassurance when your dog is sitting quietly and you are in control of the situation. Over a period, this will give him confidence and he will realise that he does not have to defend himself.*
> • *Extra reinforcement for any barking such as a water spray can be used by you (not a stranger) to quieten your dog, once you are sure he has an understanding of the command. Remember, always balance the praise appropriately as you will have introduced a more negative reinforcement.*

Aggression

Any dog has the potential to become aggressive, as this is a dog's only self-defence mechanism. Displays of body posture, eye contact, barking and growling are all warning signs that your dog will have been showing for some time.

It is very important to understand why he is being aggressive and to deal with it in the correct manner. You must avoid physical confrontation, as this will only heighten the problem. In most cases, it is advisable to seek professional help.

Physically controlling your dog at any stage will only encourage him to become aggressive, as you are setting the rules.

There are many different types of aggression: such as protective, apprehensive, dominance that can be manifested towards people, other dogs and other species. Try to establish how your dog is feeling by observing his body posture and analysing the situations in which his aggression is occurring.

For example, if he is aggressive over any particular item – food, bones, toys, his bed, your sofa or a stolen item, he is displaying protective aggression.

If he is aggressive towards strangers, in unusual or frightening situations or when he is cornered or threatened, he is showing apprehensive aggression – here he is protecting himself as he is frightened or threatened.

Aggression shown towards other dogs will either be apprehensive due to lack of socialisation or a bad experience or dominance aggression. Aggression shown towards other animals will be dominance or a natural hunting instinct.

Protective aggression

It is important with protective aggression to do some background work reversing your dog's protectiveness (see Dropping Items, p.91) as a physical battle will only cause the problem to get worse.

From an early age, it is important for all members of the family to regularly swap toys and items for food with your dog and ensure he is happy to be stroked and touched whilst he is playing with a toy or eating his food.

If a problem occurs, you can show vocal displeasure for your dog, growling over an item or food, but the dog must be rewarded for giving it up to you.

A programme of hand-feeding your dog his meal will subtly dominate him, as well as help build a positive association with your presence when eating.

• Hand-feed your dog while holding his bowl out of reach.
• Once he is happy and relaxed taking the food, move on to using two feed bowls, having an empty bowl on the floor and simply placing your dog's meal handful by handful into the bowl. Wait each time for him to look up and ask you to give him more. This will form a pleasant association of your hand going towards the bowl.
• Gradually increase the amount of food in the empty bowl and while he is eating, put your hand towards the bowl with something more exciting than his usual diet in your hand. Again, your dog will associate positively with your approach.
• Subtle domination in all other areas should be used, so he will understand his place in your pack.

Apprehensive aggression

Your dog has a critical psychological area within which he feels happy or safe. In a fear-based situation, your dog will make a choice of fight or flight (to defend himself or run away).

• It is important if your dog is apprehensive or nervous not to corner him or restrict him on a tight lead: you will only encourage him to defend himself, as then he cannot escape from the situation.
• Remember, your attitude is important to give your dog confidence. Use commands 'Quiet' and 'Sit' and vocally reassure when achieved.
• Over a period of time, with you taking control in these situations, you will give your dog more confidence so he will not feel the need to defend himself.

Dominance/animal aggression

In a case of aggression towards other dogs, animals or people it is important you are aware of the legal implications associated with this, as you could be liable for prosecution. Try to avoid problematic situations, as your dog will learn from his own behaviour.

A combination of control and socialisation can help to improve the problem in most cases, but professional help and advice should be sought.

IN THE CAR

Problems with travelling in the car are common. As dogs only learn from associations, this type of inappropriate behaviour quickly establishes into a habit.

Barking, crying, over-excitability, leaping around the seats and travel sickness are all easy to solve by reversing the association with the car and travel.

• From the beginning, decide where in the car you would like your dog to travel. A dog guard is an easy way of confining him and minimising the possibility of problems occurring. If you don't have a dog guard, tie him up initially in the car to reinforce a pattern of behaviour.

Barking

If your dog is barking in the car at passers-by through protectiveness or excitement, teaching an association with 'Quiet' is your first form of control (see Barking, p.95). If you are driving, you obviously need to concentrate on the road and your surroundings. By doing some background work at all other times when your dog is barking (when you are in close proximity to him), you will be able to reinforce your voice response to the command, thus increasing your control in the car.

Over-excitability

Using control obedience when leaving the house and prior to allowing your dog to jump into the car will help you to minimise his excitement, for example:

- *Sit/stay when putting the lead on*
- *Sit/stay as you leave your home*
- *You walk though the door first*
  then call your dog through
- *Sit/stay before allowing the dog to*
  jump in the car

If you do not have a dog guard and your dog travels on the back seat, using a lead to secure him in one area will help to establish a calm attitude in the car initially.

Travel sickness

As a dog only learns from associations, if he is travel sick from a young age, when seeing the car he will start to feel sick even before the car starts to move.

• Build a positive association with the car by feeding your dog his dinner in it, without the engine running initially, then progress to starting the car.
• Start taking your dog on very short journeys, your aim being to avoid him being sick. Try using positive destination journeys, for example, to the park as this will accelerate his pleasant association.
• Do not feed your dog prior to any journey.

Digging

Digging is a natural instinct that is related to burying and storing of excess food, therefore it can be difficult totally to eradicate.

By building your dog a digging area, you will be able to minimise the destructiveness in your garden.

* *Board off a small area in your garden and fill it with sand or soft peat as this will encourage your dog to dig there, rather than in your flower beds or lawn.*
* *Do not leave your dog unattended in the garden until you have built the correct association of where to dig.*
* *When you catch your dog digging in any unwanted area, tell him off vocally and take him to this digging area, then actively encourage him to dig. For example, bury biscuits or toys.*
* *Praise when digging in this area.*

If you are consistent about this, your dog will quickly associate where is and where is not acceptable to dig.

Nervousness

Lack of confidence or nervousness are common problems, which can manifest themselves in many different ways. Often, your dog's emotion is clearly apparent with displays of submissive body posture, panic or even growling or barking, but it may not always be so clear.

If your dog shows a change in character or is reluctant to go near any new object, person or situation, or into a different environment, this could be a sign to you he is feeling under-confident.

When a dog is apprehensive or nervous, his hackles may rise as a show of self-defence.

Other signs of under-confidence can also be inappropriate yawning, scratching or shaking. After a situation or event that has affected your dog, you could see your dog shaking (as though it is wet). This is a sign he has recovered and is resettling himself.

Nervousness is connected to your dog's own independent confidence and also his adaptability. Although he may be confident and relaxed in his home environment, this could change dramatically in different environments or situations: for example, travelling in the car or meeting different people.

The younger your dog, the more adaptable he will be. With under-confident puppies, early socialisation / habituation is very important.

• *If your dog is generally nervous in different situations or with a change in environment, gradually and regularly getting him used to these situations will help him to become more adaptable and confident. You need to do this in a controlled, positive way. Take it at your dog's pace – do not throw him in at the deep end.*
• *Take him to different areas and try to build positive associations, for example, feeding him his dinner and playing with his toys, can help to take the intensity away from the environment.*

• *Your attitude is very important – being too reassuring or over-supportive will only reinforce the behaviour he is displaying – 'Good boy to be scared' or 'Escape'. You should be confident and relaxed – the more you react the more the dog will worry.*
• *Control any panic or him attempting to escape with a 'Sit' command. Reassure and praise when doing this action.*
• *Give your dog space from the situation and gradually move him closer as he settles.*
• *Lowering the protein in his diet can also have a beneficial effect. Try homeopathic remedies for nervousness, these could help to calm him down.*

Nervousness with people

If your dog is under-confident or scared with people, this could make him either bark or back away to defend himself (see apprehensive aggression). *You* must control him, because if anyone else that he doesn't trust tries to control him, this could exaggerate the problem. Remember, encourage a confident attitude by:

> • *Controlling any barking (see barking)*
> • *Not allowing anyone to try to make friends with your dog; and you must not force him towards them. Any intensity from a person – staring at him, talking to him or standing in front of him – will intimidate him*
> • *Allowing him space, making him sit and stay*
> • *Asking people to throw food gently towards him without making eye contact*
> • *Letting him make friends in his own time*
> • *Giving him a bone or a chew when visitors arrive, remembering to remove it once they have gone. This way he will build a positive association with their presence; also his concentration will be distracted away from them, creating a more relaxing environment.*

Nervousness with other dogs

Gradually habituate and socialise your dog with other dogs. Take him to parks and on walks to allow him to interact with other dogs.

This should be done with dogs 'off the lead' as the restriction will make him more nervous and encourage him to defend himself as he can't escape – hence making the problem worse.

Remember:

• Keep a relaxed attitude yourself – try to just keep walking and don't praise or speak to him until after the encounter, as the more you make of the situation, the more your dog will react.

• If you make friends with the other dogs, this will also help, as it will give him confidence.

• Try not to over-protect your dog as he needs to learn interaction to help his independence and confidence. The more he interacts, the more he learns it's not such a big deal.

Nervousness with noises

Sound shyness is usually associated with breeds with a high hearing sensitivity such as herding or hunting breeds, although all dogs have much greater hearing intensity than our own. Sound shyness is a problem which is difficult to totally cure, but you can help your dog to cope with situations. Unseen noises such as fireworks, thunder or hot air balloons can usually cause more fear as the dog cannot relate to where the noise is coming from.

> *• Your attitude is very important; he only learns from associations in situations like this and he will be effectively scaring himself and confounding the problem*
> *• If your dog is panicking, tell him in a firm tone what he should be doing, then over a period of time this action will give him confidence – in the future he may not like the sound, but he will be able to cope with it!*
> *• If inside, tell your dog to go to his bed and praise and reassure him for staying there. Put his bed in a confined space, e.g. under the table or behind the sofa – this will help to give him more confidence.*

• If outside, command your dog to sit and stay, then reassure him for doing the action, calm him down and then resume the walk.
• If your dog is nervous of traffic or siren noises, gradually introduce him to these – taking him to a busier area and getting him to sit, letting him watch the world go by.
• Feeding him in certain situations will also help to ease your dog's nervousness. Additionally, homeopathic remedies are very effective to help calm a dog stressed or worried by noise.

INDEX